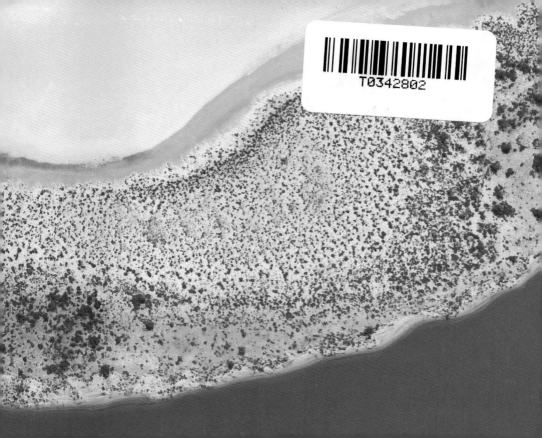

WESTERN AUSTRALIA
THE GOLDEN STATE

WESTERN AUSTRALIA

THE GOLDEN STATE

NEW HOLLAND

INTRODUCTION

Western Australia is vast and a diverse region boasting some of the most breathtaking natural wonders in the world and some of the most stunning beaches with a beautiful underwater world to explore.

The capital city is called Perth, which has over two million people living there and is known for its sunny climate, beautiful skylines with pristine beaches with great urban outdoor spaces for inner city living and the Swan River that sits along side the city's edge. The city has a vibrant cultural scene with theatres, galleries, art and music venues and a trendy cafe and food scene. As well as a buzzing bar and pub scene for a good Australian Sunday session just like the locals.

Perth was founded by Captain James Stirling in 1829 and the city is situated on the traditional lands of the Whadjuk Noongar people, where they have lived for at

least 45,000 years. Perth was named after the city of Perth in Scotland.

In the late 19th century Western Australia gold rush expanded and saw a growth in population and immigrants and in the early 21st century a successful boom in mining in various regions of Western Australia make Perth one of the major headquarters for mining operations in the world.

Kings Park and the Botanic gardens offers a panoramic view of the city and Swan River, and has lush gardens to enjoy a picnic or take a stroll and enjoy the diverse native flora and eucalyptus trees.

Perth is home to unique wildlife such as quokkas, numbats, blue-ringed octopuses, black swans, kangaroos, koalas, wallabies, and nature is right on your doorstep in Perth and throughout Western Australia.

Close to Perth there are some popular landmarks such as Kings Park and Botanic Garden, one of the largest urban parks in the world; the Fremantle Prison; Rottnest Island; Perth Zoo with over 1000 animals; and the Bell Tower offering incredible views of the city; as well as the Western Australian Museum, one of the most premier museums on natural history, Aboriginal culture and art, maritime history and lots of exhibitions throughout the year.

Some of the most stunning beaches in Perth include City Beach and Scarborough and of course Cottesloe Beach.

The economy is based on tourism, mining and agriculture and also has a number of universities.

The sunny climate means weather in Western Australia can reach record breaking heatwaves and dry conditions in summer and mild wet winters. The hottest times of the year to go to Western Australia are between December and February and the cooler months where the temperature drops are from June to August. Most people who live in Perth and Western Australia enjoy the heat and the climate for an outdoor lifestyle all year round.

The Margaret River region is world class for its wineries and the gourmet food it produces in the area that attract tourists all year round as a popular tourist destination for wine lovers and international visitors.

Further north, Ningaloo Reef offers snorkelling and diving where you can swim with sharks and explore a vibrant underwater world like no other in the world.

The Kimberley region has remote beauty only found in Western Australia covering an area of around 200,000 sq km of Western Australia with its rugged landscapes, waterfalls, rivers, gorges and coastline. It is also home to birds and other wildlife.

The Pinnacles Desert with its limestone formations is in the Nambung National Park and showcases its remarkable geological formations known as the Pinnacles. Also the ancient Bungle Bungle Range in Purnululu National Park which is a UNESCO World Heritage Site with incredible rock formations and hidden gorges and pools of water to explore with many hiking trails.

The iconic and famous Wave Rock is a giant rock formation that has shaped over millions of years from wind and water erosion and so unique to those who visit the rock. The Wave Rock Festival is a popular outdoor music festival held annually.

As you venture around Western Australia there is so much to see and do in this incredible state, not only the biggest state in Australia but the most diverse even down to a pink coloured lake located on the Middle Island off the coast of Western Australia.

Western Australia has so much to offer and is one of Australia's most beautiful states with incredible sunsets, clean and pristine beaches, amazing nature right on your doorstep to incredible history filled with rich culture and heritage.

PERTH

City skyline, Perth.

Elizabeth Quay Park, Perth.

Mitchell Freeway connecting city of Perth.

Elizabeth Quay, Perth.

Fireworks lighting up the sky over the Matagarup Bridge, Perth.

Elizabeth Quay, Perth.

Perth skyline.

Perth Stadium.

Perth Zoo.

Kangaroos at the Heirisson Island Kangaroo Sanctuary, Perth.

The State War Memorial at Kings Park and Botanic Garden, Perth.

DNA Tower in Kings Park, Perth.

Black Swan on the Swan River.

Spring wildflowers southeast of Perth near Porongurup.

A bridge in the Kings Park and Botanic Gardens.

Western Australian Botanic Garden.

The Pioneer Women's Memorial is located in the Western Australian Botanic Garden in Kings Park in Perth.

Kings Park and Botanic Garden, Perth.

Large gum nuts on a eucalyptus tree.

Kangaroo Paws and Wildflowers in Bloom at Kings Park, Perth.

Perth Mint.

Perth skyline.

Elizabeth Quay, Perth.

Perth city.

Mardalup Park and Swan River in Perth.

Dolphins along the Swan River and open seas on the ferry from Perth's CBD to Rottnest Island.

Perth skyline.

44

Male Black Swan on the shoreline of Swan River in Perth.

Four black swans on the Swan River, Perth.

Claisebrook Cove in East Perth.

Halls Head Beach, south of Perth.

Fremantle Railway Station.

Fremantle beach.

The Containbow, Fremantle.

Fremantle Markets.

Fremantle Markets.

Fremantle Goal in the day and night.

Fremantle Goal.

The Whalers Tunnel of the Round House jail at Fremantle.

Roundhouse in Fremantle.

Fishing Boat Harbour, Fremantle.

Fremantle Harbour.

Aerial view of Coogee Beach and the Omeo Shipwreck in Fremantle.

Fremantle Boat Harbour.

The Port of Fremantle.

Western Australia Shipwrecks Museum, Fremantle.

Fremantle.

Colonial 1860s Building, Fremantle.

The War Memorial at Monument Hill, Fremantle. Designed by architects and built in 1928 this memorial commemorates World War I and II, the Korean War, the Malayan Emergency and the Vietnam War.

Fremantle War Memorial.

The war memorial at Monument Hill, Fremantle.

Fremantle shipping docks.

Fremantle shipping docks.

Scarborough Beach.

Scarborough Beach.

Scarborough, Australia.

Cottesloe Beach, Perth.

Cottesloe Beach, Perth.

Perth sunset.

Common bottle-nosed dolphins (*Tursiops truncatus*) surfing in wave.

Quokka on Rottnest Island.

Quokka is enjoying his meal, Rottnest Island.

Bathurst Lighthouse on Rottnest Island.

Mary Cove at Rottnest Island.

Rottnest Island.

City Beach, Perth.

Rockingham foreshore with a jetty.

Coastal cave on the Penguin Island.

A Fairy Penguin standing near the water at Penguin Island, Rockingham.

Rockingham.

A group of Pied Cormorant.

A sea lion and a group of pelicans on the sandy beach of Penguin Island, Rockingham.

Point Peron and Shoalwater Bay.

Point Peron with Garden Island at Rockingham.

Busselton Jetty.

Busselton Jetty.

Busselton Jetty in Busselton.

The rocks in the canal off the coast in Busselton.

Misery Beach, Albany.

The Gap in Albany.

Margaret River skyline.

Kookaburra at Margaret River.

Castle Rock, Dunsborough, Margaret River.

Margaret River.

Margaret River.

Meelup Beach in Dunsborough.

Yallingup.

Canal Rocks in Yallingup, between the towns of Dunsborough and Margaret River.

Lake Cave, Margaret River.

Western Grey Kangaroo, Margaret River.

Boranup Karri forest near Margaret River.

Dolphins swimming in crystal clear water in Margaret River.

Hutt Lagoon Pink Lake, Port Gregory.

Hutt Lagoon, pink saltwater lake at Port Gregory.

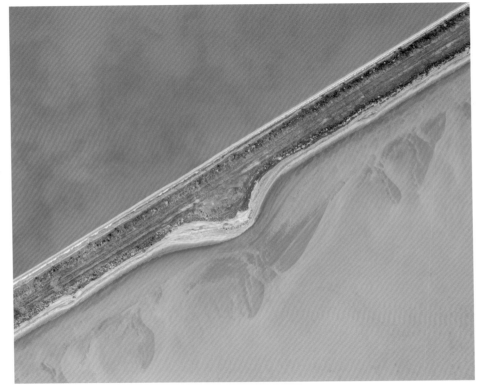

Hutt Lagoon, Port Gregory.

Lucky Bay, Cape Le Grand National Park.

The industrial port of Esperance.

Wharton Beach in Esperance.

Kangaroo family.

Kangaroo family at the beach in Esperance.

Sea Lion in Esperance.

Echidna foraging at 11 Mile Beach, Esperance.

Seagull at the Esperance.

Twlight Cove Lookout, Esperance.

Salt Lake in the Goldfields-Esperance region.

Kalgoorlie is in the goldfields region.

Cave Hill near Kalgoorlie.

Kalgoorlie.

Kalgoorlie Goldfields.

Inside the giant Super Pit Kalgoorlie.

Kalgoorlie road sign.

Kalgoorlie-Boulder City.

Dolphins in Monkey Mia.

Shell Beach, Monkey Mia.

Sea turtle in Monkey Mia.

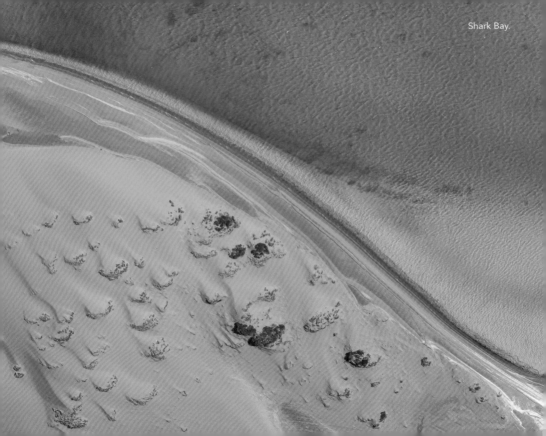
Shark Bay.

Shark Bay.

Francois Peron National Park in Shark Bay.

Charles Knife Canyon, Exmouth.

Emu in the bushland near Exmouth.

Jurabi Coastal Park, Ningaloo Coast, Exmouth, one of the most important nesting places of sea turtles in WA.

Baby turtles at Exmouth.

177

A humpback whale in Exmouth.

Mobula ray.

Purple Mulla Mulla in the Cape Range National Park.

Sturt Desert Pea.

Ningaloo Reef near Exmouth.

Schooling Grey Reef Sharks, Ningaloo Reef.

Whale Shark, Ningaloo Reef.

Humpback Whales, Exmouth.

A large grouper under the Navy pier in Exmouth.

A termite mound in Exmouth.

Charles Knife canyon near Exmouth, Ningaloo.

Rock-wallaby.

Highway between Exmouth and Coral Bay.

Cape Leveque near Broome.

Lucky Bay in Cape Le Grand National Park.

James Price Point, Kimberley, Broome.

Willie Creek, Broome, Kimberley.

Sandy Cable Beach, Broome.

Camels on the shore of Cable Beach, Broome.

Cable Beach, Broome.

Broome.

Cave at Gantheaume Point, Broome.

Kimberley.

Red Sand Beach, Roebuck Bay, Broome.

Mitchell Falls, Kimberley.

Red Pindan Cliffs at James Price Point, Kimberley.

Horizontal Falls in the Kimberley.

Bungle Bungle National Park, Purnululu, Kimberley.

Cockburn Range. Kimberley.

Windjana Gorge, Kimberley.

Gibb River Road, Kimberley.

Horizontal Falls in the islands of the Kimberley.

Simpsons Beach, Broome, Kimberley.

Gibb River, Kimberley.

Gibb River, Kimberley.

Wolfe Creek Crater, Kimberley.

An old quarry near Fitzroy Crossing along the Gibb River Road.

Wave Rock, Hyden.

Kangaroo and it's family.

Thorny devils are found in the arid and semi-arid regions of Western Australia.

Yalgoo, a gold mining town in the midwest of WA.

Parry Range, Pilbara, Ashburton Shire, in the remote outback.

The giant Elachbutting Rock, Great Western Woodlands.

A red dirt road through the middle of the desert in Karijini National Park.

Pinnacles Desert at Nambung National Park.

Nature's Window, Kalbarri National Park.

Pilbara.

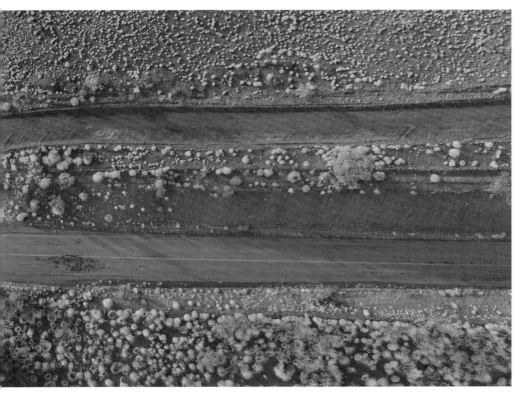

Rufous Whistler in the bushland of the Swan Valley.

Stromatolites in Hamelin Pool, Shark Bay.

Cathedral Gorge Cave in the Purnululu National Park.

Communications tower at Gantheaume Point, Broome.

Hawk Eagle in the Kimberley.

Red-tailed black cockatoo, Swan Valley, Perth.

Python.

Wild goat on red cliff, Kimberley.

First published in 2025 by New Holland Publishers
Sydney

Level 1, 178 Fox Valley Road, Wahroonga, NSW 2076, Australia

newhollandpublishers.com

Copyright © 2025 New Holland Publishers
Copyright © 2025 in images: New Holland Image Library, Shutterstock, Adobe Stock
and various others credited.

A record of this book is held at the National Library of Australia.

ISBN 9781760792053

Managing Director: Fiona Schultz
General Manager/Publisher: Olga Dementiev
Designer: Andrew Davies
Production Director: Arlene Gippert
Printed in China

Keep up with New Holland Publishers:

 NewHollandPublishers

 @newhollandpublishers